Haunted Dartmoor

Margaret Caine and
Alan Gorton

Picture Credits
Cover image: © Shutterstock
Tree image: © Shutterstock
All other photographs: © Margaret Caine 2014

Designed by Alix Wood: www.alixwood.co.uk

Published by Orchard Publications
Orchard is an imprint of Tor Mark,
United Downs Ind Est, Redruth,
Cornwall TR16 5HY

First Published 2014

Text © Margaret Caine & Alan Gorton 2014

ISBN 978 1898964 94 0

Printed by Hedgerow Print, Marsh Lane,
Lords Meadow, Crediton EX17 1ES

Lewtrenchard Manor – EX20 4PN

Hidden in a wooded hollow beneath the wild tors on the north-western edge of Dartmoor, the original Lewtrenchard manor was recorded in the Domesday Book as a Royal manor leased by the Sheriff of Devon to his relative Rogeries de Moles for a rent of £4. Later, in 1327 at the beginning of the reign of Henry III, the Trenchard family took it over, and silver coins from this time have been found in the walls and below the floors.

Through marriage into the Trenchards, the estate was inherited by the Monk family of nearby Potheridge. They were a colourful lot. One of them, Sir Thomas Monk got himself into such serious financial difficulties in 1623 that he was thrown into a debtors' prison in Exeter. To pay off what he could, in 1626 he sold the property to Henry Gould, a successful banker. Henry had married Ann Williams, and you can see their initials carved into the ornate overmantle in the front hall. They also brought the motto 'GOOLD BYDETH EVER BRIGHT'. It is with their descendants that the property is linked most indelibly. We are left with their ghosts.

One, named The White Lady, is Susannah Gould who on March 19, 1729, was married in the local church. It was not, for her, as happy a day as it might have been. Her father Edward, the third son of Henry and Ann, had inherited in 1667, and he and his wife Elizabeth had two daughters. Anna had married well but Henry did not approve of Susannah's chosen groom, Peter Truscott, nor his family, and refused to attend the wedding. As she was walking alone up the drive after the ceremony, Susannah suddenly felt faint, let out an agonised gasp, collapsed into her new husband's arms as he rushed towards her and died from heart failure (some say she was poisoned because of the feud between the families). Such a tragic end to the day left its mark. Her forlorn ghost drifts sadly along the drive where the tragedy occurred, still dressed in her wedding gown, or quietly through the lower fields as recently as 2001.

Unfortunately, not all the family members were so successful in business as Henry Gould. Subsequent owners squandered his fortune. Not for nothing was Captain Edward Gould nicknamed 'the Scamp', and seems to have made a valiant attempt to get rid of the family's wealth. A compulsive gambler, he was not averse to resorting to desperate measures to recoup his losses. On one occasion when he lost heavily at cards he disguised himself as a highwayman, ambushed the man who had won his money, and shot him when the man resisted. Brought to trial, he was defended by an astute young barrister named James Dunning. In court, the sole witness to the murder said he recognised the defendant in the moonlight. With a flourish, Dunning produced an almanac from his coat pocket which showed that there had been no moon on the night in question. But he didn't reveal that the almanac had been specially printed. 'The Scamp' was found not guilty. Unfortunately, the heavy costs of the trial left him penniless and he died in poverty in 1777, only eleven years after inheriting the estate. Fortunately for the Manor, his mother Margaret, nee Belfield, who had married William Drake Gould in 1740, took over. She knew what her son Edward was like and had granted him a 90-year mortgage on the property, which she now took up. She was an amazing business woman: not only did she restore the family finances and repay all the debts but put the estate back on its feet and improved the house. Because of the fondness this spirited matriarch had for Lewtrenchard and its dependants, and the deep respect in which she was held, as well as some indication of her character, she was affectionately known as 'Old Madam'.

After she died on 10 April 1795 in her ninetieth year, she simply couldn't bear to leave her beloved Manor. In fact, she had refused to die in bed. She just sat in a chair by the fire as she finally drifted off. At the very moment she breathed her last, every window shutter and door in the house flew open and within an hour her ghost was appearing to people within the house and to a farm hand who saw her under a walnut tree in the grounds. Less than an hour later, a tenant farmer coming to pay his respects was startled to see the unmistakable figure of 'Old Madam' striding up the drive towards him: she paid him no attention but marched straight past towards the church. A week later a man named Symonds saw her in a field by the River Lew. 'Old Madam' was sitting on a plough and waved to him. He had just returned from America and wasn't aware she was dead! Many people saw her after that. She appeared to people walking on Galford Down, not far away, but nothing quite as dramatic as the events that occurred on a dull day in 1832. A carpenter working on the church had heard of 'Old Madam' Gould's ghostly wandering so decided to peer inside her vault. She was not amused! She rose out of her grave, chased the startled man out of the church, across a field and all the way to his home. He didn't have to look behind. Her ghost gave out such a bright light that it cast a shadow over him as he ran. Now her ghost walks around the house, particularly the Long Gallery and the landing corridor on the first floor, making sure all is well with the property she so loved. She appears whenever damage is done – merely the breaking of a window is sufficient to cause 'Old Madam' to walk again!

Apparently, 'Old Madam' was particularly fond of children. When children staying in the hotel have felt unwell, she has appeared to see how they are and to make sure they are being cared for. On those occasions, she appears as a smiling old lady, usually in a dark coloured dress.

Through marriage, the family became the Baring-Goulds. Their coat of arms is in the stained glass windows and on the ornate plasterwork of the ceilings. 'Old Madam' brought about the change in name. When her daughter Margaret married Charles Baring, 'Old Madam' disapproved of his 'strange' religious beliefs and was determined they would never inherit Lewtrenchard. She arranged that it would pass to their son, her grandson, William Baring, on condition he added 'Gould' to his name.

Sabine Baring-Gould was of a different mould, one of the most gentle of men. Born in 1834, he went on to become a prolific author, celebrated antiquarian, eminent folklorist, hymn writer and traveller (his desk still stands in the front hall), as well as both the local squire and local vicar. His father threatened to disinherit him if he took holy orders and it was not until 1871 that father relented because of the deteriorating mental health of his younger brother, Willy. Sabine was prepared to risk all by entering the Church but managed to persuade his parents he was not cut out to be a mathematics teacher although he did have a paid appointment at St John's College, Hurstpierpoint, from 1857 to 1864. He also taught in a choir school in Pimlico but again his Low Church father disapproved of this High Church association. Sabine's first curacy was in Yorkshire, where he composed 'Onward Christian Soldiers' to encourage his parishioners to climb the steep hill to the church on Sundays. It is also where he met 16-years-old Grace Taylor, a mill girl. After making sure she had had an education, for which he paid, he married her. Tongues wagged, but the couple remained happily together for 48 years and produced 15 children. When he inherited the estates, he managed to arrange a transfer to take up the living at Lewtrenchard, where he undertook restoration of the parish church which had not had much money spent on it since the 1520s. Like his ancestor Margaret, Sabine Baring-Gould too loved the Manor and until he died in 1924 used his prodigious energy to transform the house into the wonderful manor of today and keep it in impeccable condition. Like Margaret, he couldn't part with it and his ghost still wanders the grounds, making sure everything is taken care of. Mostly though, he seems to be simply standing and enjoying his surroundings, which he largely created. Today, the Grade II listed Jacobean-style house is a country hotel, full of memories – and ghosts.

Wonson Manor – EX20 2JA

W onson Manor is tucked away from curious (or prying) eyes, behind huge gates and high walls. It has been here for many years. It began life as a Norman fortified manor, and parts of the present fabric date back to the twelfth century though it was extensively renovated and restyled during the seventeenth, and is now listed Grade II*. For many years, the manor and its estate were owned by the Northmore family, leading Tory gentry in the area – and through them has acquired not one but two ghosts.

Open the door carefully and very quietly and you will see four men, playing cards. Why? They are a legacy of the time in September 1722 when William Northmore, MP for Okehampton between 1713 and 1734, and an addicted gambler, put up the deeds of the estate as a stake and lost the family fortune on the throw of a single card – the ace of diamonds. As a permanent reminder of just how foolish he had been, he had an enormous 6ft x 6ft ace of diamonds painted on one of the panels of the wainscot in the upstairs gaming room, which he turned into his bedroom. Each night, he cursed it. The whole incident had such a profound effect on him that he never touched another card. However, his ill fortune certainly had a permanent influence on the place. Oddly, the men are dressed as cavaliers. We don't know why: perhaps they just liked that style of dress or admired a previous generation. However, none of them seem to be connected with the other apparition, a friendly lady who smooths guests' pillows and tucks them into bed. It's a homely touch but some visitors find it disconcerting!

Some 4,000 years ago, the prehistoric people who lived on the high moor at Scorhill created a stone circle 80 feet in diameter. We can only guess why the place was important to them as they carried and set up the 60 huge boulders, though it may have been for some form of communal ritual. Many hundreds of years later, the place took on another focus – and a ghost. Here, unfaithful wives or promiscuous young girls from Wonson, Gidleigh and surrounding villages were publicly humiliated. First, any accused woman had to bathe naked in Cranmere pool near Okehampton. Then, dressed only in a shirt they were walked to the River Teign at Gidleigh to bathe again. Next they were taken to the Scorhill stone circle where they had to kneel in front of the tallest stone and beg forgiveness for their sins. If nothing happened, the woman was deemed forgiven. There were occasions however when the stone toppled over and crushed the woman to death. Tradition says that the dozen or so stones lying on the ground are evidence of this punishment. It is one of those unfortunate women who now returns in ghostly form. This Grey Lady of Gidleigh walks, head bowed, from the Teign up the banks of Blackawton Brook – though an alternative story is that she drowned herself in the river rather than endure the shame.

Brook Manor – TQ11 0HR

$\mathbb{E}$ach year, thousands of visitors come to Buckfast Abbey. Few even notice its neighbour, the forlorn, hollow shell of what was Holy Trinity church. Do go to see it. As you walk up the path you will notice a building outside the south porch. Some visitors think it's a sort of kiosk, others a prison, and they're not far wrong. In fact, it is a strange mausoleum – known locally as the 'sepulchre' – in which the remains of the Cabell family are incarcerated and, importantly for us, Squire Richard Cabell. Peer through the metal bars and you'll see that the tomb has a gigantic white slab on top of it. Clearly, this is not the normal family burial plot. Somebody was trying to ensure whoever is inside didn't get out. But that was only the beginning of the story.

Three miles up a long valley running deep into Dartmoor is Brook Manor. Here lived Richard Cabell. We know a little about him. He was the local squire, had a passion for hunting and an entry in *The House of Commons Journal* for 1647 reports that '*Squire Richard Cabell of Buckfastleigh in the County of Devon*' was fined by Parliament for taking the Royalist side in the Civil War. Later, he retracted his support for Charles I and was pardoned. Undoubtedly, this upset local people whose livelihood depended on the Duchy of Cornwall and perhaps this is why malicious stories about him began to spread – that he lived immorally and that he was in league with the Devil. No wonder he was recorded as a '*monstrously evil man*'. We also know from church records that he married Elizabeth Fowell at Ugborough on 7 January 1654/55, that they had one daughter, that he rebuilt part of his house, inscribing the date 1656 and his initials 'R C' on it, and that people said he had a predilection for village maidens. The rumour was that having captured one, he would keep her under lock and key at Hawson Manor on the other side of the valley, presumably hidden from Mrs Cabell. So he acquired an unenviable reputation as an unprincipled, violent and powerful squire, scaring the local populace, and when he came to die his end was not pleasant. One version says that as he lay ill a pack of spectral black hounds, Wisht Hounds, came baying from the depths of Dartmoor and gathered round the house, howling horribly, to escort his soul to hell. Another says that he was out hunting and the Wisht Hounds chased him across the moor until he dropped dead from exhaustion. In yet a third version, he reputedly accused his wife of adultery, and in a fit of temper beat her savagely. She fled onto the moor but he caught and murdered her, stabbing her with his hunting knife. In her defence, her faithful pet hound flew at him and ripped out his throat, as both fell to their deaths: many say its pitiful howls can still be heard at night on the moor, and that it re-appears to every generation of the Cabell family. In fact, Cabell's wife outlived him by some fourteen years: she is recorded as 'Mrs Elizabeth Cabel' who was buried in linen on 17 September 1686 – but nevertheless the legend has persisted.

So when the Squire passed away on July 5, 1677, locals were convinced there would be ghostly reprisals. They made sure he was buried deeper than usual with a heavy stone on his coffin inside a solid altar tomb inside a square-shaped building with an iron grille (on the assumption that ghosts and vampires cannot pass iron): hopefully this would at least contain his 'unquiet spirit' and he would never trouble them again.

We now know that the villagers' precautions came to naught. They had reason to be scared. Things really started to happen straight away. On the night of his interment, the hellish pack of hounds came baying across the moor to howl and shriek at his new tomb. Ever since, he has been seen leading this phantom pack and, if they are not out hunting in full cry across the windswept moor, they are wailing around his grave, filling the air with unearthly howling. Despite all the villagers' efforts, his tormented spirit still doesn't rest.

But we must ask: how did the legends surrounding Richard Cabell arise? Can we separate historical fact from folk-lore? It's rather complicated. The first known Richard Cabell came to Devon from Frome, Somerset, to marry a Susan Peter who lived at Wallaford, near Buckfastleigh. They had a son, also Richard, who was educated at Exeter College, Oxford, and later at the Inns of Court. He in turn married the daughter of a wealthy Exeter merchant called Prestwood, and quickly began to expand the Cabell family's estates by buying surrounding land. It is most likely this Richard Cabell who took up the Royalist cause and had to pay heavy fines to retain possession of his home, Brook Manor. He also had a son, yet another Richard, who also attended Exeter College and the Inns of Court, though the Civil War interrupted his studies. The father Richard died in 1655, and shortly afterwards this third Richard married Elizabeth Fowell, daughter of Sir Edward Fowell who was President of the Committee of Sequestration – the person responsible for the huge fines imposed on his father. Should we be surprised that there was a reversal of fortune and that after his marriage the Cabell family's estates, including Brook Manor, were restored to this new husband and son-in-law? Nonetheless, he was never a popular person in the

Buckfastleigh area. This third Richard had no male heir, so on his death in July, 1677, the Cabell estates were inherited by his daughter, also Elizabeth. In 1693, she married Cholmeley D'Oyly, one of 12 children of the impoverished Sir John D'Oyly, and made a generous marriage settlement of £10,000 on her new husband. Seven years later, Cholmeley died. Only then did Elizabeth discover he had not been exactly honest with her: he had already been married to an even more impoverished vicar's daughter! So Elizabeth set out to overturn the settlement and recover her £10,000, claiming that her marriage was not lawful. It was a long and complex case which resulted in the first Mrs D'Oyly's marriage being declared invalid. Elizabeth got her money back, but in doing so incurred heavy costs for the Chancery case and subsequent appeal. Later, Elizabeth remarried, to Richard Fownes of Dorset ,where she went to live. When his parents died, this Richard had to sell his house to settle his parents' debts and the couple moved back to Brook Manor.

So are the stories regarding Squire Richard Cabell actually an amalgam consisting of the second and third Richard and Cholmeley his bigamous son-in-law, all combined with a general dislike of the family because of their actions in the Civil War and afterwards, and which evolved into a characterisation so evil that he haunts the area with his devil dogs?

We may probably never know. But we do know the notoriously evil Squire who had quarrelled with all his neighbours at one time or another still visits Brook Manor, along an ancient track known as Abbot's Way. You can see him on the anniversary of his death each July 5 lashing his huge horse to ever greater speed up the steep, narrow, twisting drive of his former house, followed by his hounds, until he reaches the churchyard where he was buried. And he became the prototype for the wicked 'Black' Hugo in Arthur Conan Doyle's dramatic thriller *The Hound of the Baskervilles*.

Whiddon Park, Chagford

– TQ13 8DG

C arved into a stone slab in the chancel floor of Chagford parish church is an epitaph:

Mary Whiddon, daughter of Oliver Whiddon, who died in 1641
Reader, would'st though know who here is laid,
Behold a matron, yet a maid
A modest look, a pious heart
A Mary for the better part
But dry thine eyes, why wilt thou weep
Such damselles do not die, but sleep.

We know a little about Mary Whiddon. During the 17th century, she lived with her family at Whiddon House and was a descendent of Justice of the Queen's Bench Sir John Whiddon (or Whyddon), who died in 1575, a man of influence and wealth who, to indicate his social standing, built the Deer Park adjacent to his property. She was also the sister of Rowland Whiddon, a Justice of the Peace during the Commonwealth interregnum who rebuilt the Elizabethan house, putting the date 1649 above the door. But Mary had already been dead for eight years by then.

Her death is a sad tale, so unusual that it was adapted by R D Blackmore into his famous story *Lorna Doone*, thinly disguised by a change of location to Exmoor. So what happened?

Young Mary, a pretty, vivacious, lively girl had two admirers. The first was a morose, introverted local man, who preferred his own company and was regarded by the villagers as something of a misfit. The other was an outgoing, friendly young fellow who many thought was destined to be a success in the world. But Mary had to choose. Encouraged by her family, she chose the latter. For the man who regarded himself as being 'jilted', it was hard to bear. Day after day he brooded in a deep, black sulk and as the weeks passed his unbearable jealousy turned to a malicious hatred of Mary. At every opportunity he would viciously malign her until in the end even the local folk's initial sympathy turned against him.

Eventually, Mary and the new man in her life announced the date for their marriage: October 11, 1641. The banns were read, the news spread and quickly filtered down to her 'jilted' lover. We don't know what his immediate reaction was, but we do know it didn't improve his mood or stop him slandering Mary. His anger must have reached fever-pitch.

The day of the wedding arrived and the excited bride and her party made their way to the little church, bringing approving gasps from the assembled villagers. Mary walked confidently up the path to the large wooden doors and down the aisle. Waiting for her at the altar was her groom, smiling lovingly. The ceremony passed without a hitch and the man and wife, their arms locked, strolled slowly along the nave, passing their families and friends, and out onto the church steps. Without warning, a loud bang rent the air, a thick purple plume of smoke wafted high into that cold October morning. Time stood still. Nobody moved. Nobody spoke. Mary crumpled onto the stone steps. A bright red stain slowly trickled over her silk wedding dress from a small hole above her heart. After the initial shock, her new husband gathered her lifeless corpse, sobbing, cradling her in his arms trying to restore her life. We don't know what happened to the murderer – her first suitor – but, so cruelly struck down, Mary was buried beneath the chancel of the church she had just been married in.

We must though question whether this murder ever really happened. Mary's epitaph states that she died '*matron, yet a maid*', which could be interpreted as 'married but unconsummated'. On the other hand 'maid' was a common term in Devon for a girl, and the inscription may mean that Mary died young (ie 'although married, still just a girl'). The only contemporaneous record we can find is her will, and that doesn't help us solve the mystery. It gives no clue to where and when it was made but she bequeathed monies to her brothers and sisters, to her godchildren, to the poor of Chagford and to the labourers of the parish. She also left a gold ring to her mother. There is no mention of any husband. It may even have been written before her marriage.

Notwithstanding this, Mary has not rested. In 1971, on the morning of her own wedding in the same parish church, a daughter of the owners at Whiddon Park House awoke to find an apparition of a young woman standing in the bedroom doorway, dressed in a period wedding gown. Fortunately, this recent bride didn't consider it any sort of omen and went ahead as planned – but she did place her bridal bouquet on Mary Whiddon's grave as a mark of respect. This followed the tradition which arose soon after Mary's burial for newly-weds to lay a flower on her memorial stone. So we know that Mary's spirit still haunts the house around dawn, still in her wedding dress. She has also been seen in the churchyard, walking towards the church.

Three Crowns Inn, Chagford

~ TQ13 8AJ

No sooner had the village of Chagford recovered from Mary Whiddon's murder than it was again enveloped in tragedy, only two years later.

On February 7, 1643, a small body of Parliamentarian forces stopped overnight at Chagford. Their welcome had been muted. Mostly, Chagford supported the Royalists because of its preferential treatment as a stannary town. The officers stayed in Whyddon House, now the Three Crowns Hotel but which had been the Whyddon family home for over 300 years. An equally small group of Cavalier horse and dragoons was moving in the same direction. Amongst them was thirty-three-year-old Sydney Godolphin. He was from an old, influential Cornish family, a courtier, talented poet and politician, MP for Helston, who had rushed to the King's support after his standard had been raised in Nottingham on August 22, 1642. But Sydney Godolphin was a *"soft and gentle man"* with no experience of war, especially the harsh realities of Civil War, *"as absolute a piece of virtue as ever our Nation bred"*, according to his commanding officer. At daybreak on February 8, the Cavaliers arrived in Chagford, surprising the Parliamentarians just as they were preparing to leave. Bullets were exchanged, Sydney Godolphin was hit by a round of musket shot and seriously wounded, just above his knee. He was carried into the large granite porch and bled to death on the cold, stone bench. Three days later he was buried amongst the great and the good in Westminster Abbey.

But time moved on. The sombre ghost of the tragic Sidney Godolphin returned to haunt the porch where he fell mortally wounded, and also to walk along a landing in the hotel, resplendent in full flamboyant Cavalier dress with a handsome plumed hat. Those who have seen him are impressed by his *piece de resistance* of walking through the thick, solid granite walls by the huge fireplace.

Even as Sydney Godolphin was bleeding to death, the running fighting continued between the bridge over the River Teign and Blackaton Brook at the bottom of Providence Hill. By the end of the morning, several men had been killed and were quickly buried in the surrounding hedges. Those wounded made their way back to Chagford as best they could. Ever since, on the anniversary of February 8 each year, you can hear the sounds of the ghostly skirmish, men shouting and screaming, horses thundering past, the clash of sword on sword.

Kilworthy House, Tavistock
– PL19 0JN

A t the far end of a long, narrow lane in Trelawney Road, Tavistock, you will come across Kilworthy House. It is home to a multitude of ghosts and appears to be one of those incident-prone houses we occasionally come across. It was built in the 16th and 17th centuries by successive members of the Glanville family as a large three-storey mansion, but after a disastrous fire was left derelict for many years before being rebuilt in its present, more modest form, and is now used as an education centre. The events which gave rise to one of its ghosts took place in the early years of the house when it belonged to Judge John Glanville, who became MP for Tavistock in 1586.

Legend tells us that Eulalia Page was the judge's daughter, that after an unpleasant forced marriage she murdered her husband and that her father presided at her trial and sentenced her to death. But there is considerable discrepancy between fiction and fact.

Eulalia Glanville was not the daughter of the judge but of a Tavistock merchant, Nicholas Glanville. She did live at Kilworthy House with her parents but they didn't own it. It belonged to her father's brother, Eulalia's uncle John, who was then serjeant-at-law, before becoming a Justice of the Common Pleas in 1598. Eulalia was deeply in love with a handsome young Naval lieutenant on a man-o'-war, George Stanwich or Strangwidge, and it is possible they were privately engaged – certainly she considered herself formally attached to him. They corresponded frequently and at first her father thought highly of Stanwich, even considering offering him a share in his business. However, for some reason he changed his mind, disapproved of their friendship, considered the young man unworthy of his daughter and began to intercept their letters. Instead, he proposed Eulalia should marry a business acquaintance, a merchant and goldsmith John Page, who was much older than Eulalia and already a widower.

John Page lived in a tall, gabled house on Woolster Street, Plymouth, which later became the Mayoralty Building, where the Guildhall now stands, and promised Nicholas Glanville he would settle "a good jointure" on Eulalia. Her father may have been influenced too by the fact he was considering moving to Plymouth himself and would be near her. Eulalia objected strongly. While nowadays we may regard a forced marriage as an unpleasant side of Elizabethan life, in certain social classes it wasn't uncommon for a young girl to be compelled to marry a rich and elderly man. Eventually, as happened, the combined efforts of Eulalia's father and mother won the day: Eulalia gave in. She immediately wrote a tear-drenched letter to Stanwich, begging him to find a way out for her. However, as she didn't get a reply she thought she had been abandoned and so married John Page.

Always referred to as 'Wealthy Page', John Page was widely regarded as a *"mean and noxious fellow"*. It was said he married solely to produce an heir so he could disappoint his own relatives who had assumed until then they would inherit his wealth. Page quickly showed his true colours. Realising he could save servants' wages, he dismissed his own staff and made his new wife and her personal maid do all the household chores – to him, his wife was in fact just another servant. In quick succession, Eulalia conceived two children but both were still-born. After the second she took opportunity to move out of the matrimonial bedroom and into her own chamber.

Now, George Stanwich came back on the scene. He contacted Eulalia, insisting he had replied to all the letters he had received, and his feelings for her were just as before. So what could they do to get out of this predicament? Some-one, possibly Eulalia's maid, suggested they "get rid of" the old husband. This they were reluctant to consider, especially Stanwich, but after seeing at first hand just how distressed Eulalia was, he agreed. But how? Eulalia may have tried to poison her hated husband as a pamphlet written soon after the event tells of how he *"was caused to vomit blood and much corruption"*. Certainly use of poison was widely known and was sometimes successful. However, Eulalia's attempt didn't work, so she offered a servant, Robert Priddis (or Prideaux), £140 to murder her husband. According to contemporary accounts she *"so corrupted him ... that he solemnly undertook and vowed to performe the task to her contentment."* This was a considerable sum of money. One can gauge the value of the bribe by comparing it with the 12d which the Mayor of Exeter ordered to be given to the bear baiter on December 17, 1586. For his part, Stanwich paid a friend, Tom Stone, to become involved also.

From records, it is possible to piece together the sequence of events. One very cold night, Wednesday, February 9, 1591, Eulalia led Priddis and Stone to her husband's bedroom, where they brutally assaulted and killed him. The pair then laid Page on his bed and arranged the bedclothes to look as if nothing untoward had happened, before Priddis went quietly to Eulalia's own bedroom to tell her that the deed had been done. About an hour later, he went to his mistress's bedroom again, this time knocking loudly and shouting for her to come to his master's room as he thought he had heard a groan – obviously a tactic to deceive the staff. Eulalia called her maid, who seems to have had no idea what was going on, and sent her into the bedroom. The girl felt her master's face which was *"as cold as clay"* and his body stiff.

Eulalia then sent Priddis to call her father, and another servant to fetch Page's sister, Mrs Harris, as her brother *"had palsy and may not live long"* It was Mrs Harris who noticed spots of blood on the corpse's chest. She immediately reported her suspicions to the Mayor and he in turn informed the other *"worshipful of the town"*: they watched as Page's body was examined. The surgeon reported *"livid finger marks around the corpse's throat, blood on his attire from scratching at his throat, plus multiple bruises and scratches on the body"* and concluded that Page had fought at least two men as they tried first to strangle him before laying him across his bed and breaking his neck. All agreed John Page had been murdered.

While all this was going on, Stanwich was having second thoughts. During the night, he went to Page's house to prevent the murder and tried to attract Eulalia's attention by throwing small stones against her window. A neighbour living opposite was disturbed by the sound, got up and saw and overheard "a young gentleman" call out *"For God's sake, stay your hand"*, to which a female replied, *"'Tis too late, the deed is done."* When this lady heard the following morning that Page had died during the night, she too reported what she had witnessed to the Mayor.

The Mayor had Priddis arrested and held in prison. He in turn implicated Tom Stone (there is a story that Stone had actually married that day and was arrested during the celebrations). Eulalia's involvement was suspected and she was cross-examined in front of the sheriff, the Mayor and other magistrates, but *"she denied not the same but said she would rather dye with Stanwich than to lieu with Page."* Part of the evidence against Eulalia was that she had apparently *"sworn she would never bear a child of his* [Page's] *getting that should prosper; which argued a most ungodly mind in this woman, for in that sort she had been the death of two of her children."* Stanwich was arrested and confessed. In mitigation he presented a letter telling the others not to go ahead, but this was not accepted as the murder had happened before the letter had arrived.

The four were committed for trial at the next Assize. Normally this would have been in Exeter but transferred to Barnstaple as plague had broken out. Memories were still fresh of the 'Black Assize' in Exeter in 1586, when the judge, eight justices and all the jury except one fell victims to 'gaol fever'. Plague recurred frequently and the organisers of the Assize had to be careful. Barnstaple itself was not immune. On October 17, 1580, Mary Feres and Joan Allen had died there of the plague, and Philip Wyot, town clerk of Barnstaple from 1586 to 1608, recorded that in 1590 the Assize had been held at Honiton and Great Torrington, *"the plague being much at Exeter"*. Wyot also gave extensive details of the 1591 Assize at Barnstaple: the presiding judge was *"Lord Anderson who tried all the cases and gave judgment upon those who were to be executed"*. After the Assize, according to Wyott, *"the gibbet was set up on the Castle Green and xvii prisoners hanged, whereof iiij of Plymouth for a murder."* It was Saturday, February 20, 1591. The parish register gives their names:

> "Here ffolloweth the names of the Prysoners wch were Buryed in the Church yeard of Barnistaple ye syce [assize] week.
> George Strongewithe, Buryed the Xxth daye
> Thomas Stone, Buryed the Xxth daye
> Robert Preidyox, Buryed at Bishopstawton ye Xxth daye"

We do not know whether Eulalia was among this mass public hanging. There is no reference to her. Because under the law killing a husband was deemed petty treason, Eulalia could have been burned alive and even 'drawn' beforehand, but there is no evidence this happened to her. By then, there was considerable revulsion against burning women to death and the executioner was allowed to strangle the condemned woman before the fire was lit. It was not until 1790 that the practice was stopped. We can only speculate what happened to Eulalia. If she was executed in this way, she would not have been the last in Devon. As late as 1750, Elizabeth Packard was burned to death at Exeter for murdering her husband. On July 29, 1782, a poor girl of only fifteen years of age, Rebecca Downing, was burnt at Heavitree, Exeter, for poisoning her master, an apothecary to whom she had been apprenticed.

Eulalia's uncle John Glanville had been at the Assize. He was listed by Wyot among the lawyers present as *'Sergt Glandyl lodging at Roy Cades'*. As such, he may even have defended his niece. We know he also witnessed her execution, by whatever means. Tradition has it that he never smiled again.

We do know that Eulalia was buried in the churchyard at Bishops Tawton. The register confirms *'Vlayia Payge daughter of Nicholas Glanville'* was interred on March 20, 1590 (NB: using the Julian Calendar). If Eulalia was burned alive, we can picture the scene. On Thursday, March 19, 1591, the pretty, dark-haired 21-year-old is dragged through the streets, pitifully calling out for her lover. George Stanwich couldn't hear. It wasn't that he was too far away – he had dangled from the end of a rope a month earlier, his disjointed corpse buried without ceremony. At the appointed place, Eulalia is tied to a stake, faggots of wood piled around her and set alight. Watched by a growing crowd, she suffers incomprehensible pain as her body melts in the flames. Death is indeed a blessed relief. But what was buried at Bishop Tawton: ashes from the fire or her body after hanging? The church warden didn't say.

Now, though, Eulalia's ghost haunts neither the site of her death nor her resting place but the terrace at the top of a steep flight of steps of Kilworthy House. She is always dressed in white and is very busy, poor soul.

Fitzford, Tavistock

- PL19 8AU

E very night for over 350 years, the gates to Fitzford have creaked open. A huge black dog bounds out, one eye red, the other black piercing the darkness, glowing ferociously. Following is a large horse-drawn coach. This is no ordinary carriage, not even an anachronism. It is a macabre, ghostly vehicle made by Satan himself from the bones of four dead men, their bleached skulls forming the corners. Alongside lopes the spectral hound, baying and howling in tones alternating from mortal anguish to evil aggression. Inside you may catch a glimpse of the ashen face of a woman. She is Lady Mary Howard, rushing towards Okehampton Park, sixteen miles away, which along with Walreddon Manor formed part of her estate. The coach rattles speedily along the old route on the western borders of Dartmoor even in the worst of weather, passing the notorious Lydford Gaol. At Okehampton Castle, Lady Mary plucks a single blade of grass. The spectral procession turns and heads back to Fitzford where she lays the grass on a stone. The spectres vanish to whence they came. The whole macabre scene is repeated next night. Lady Mary's torment must continue until every blade is plucked, and at that point, legend tells us, the world will end. But be careful. Seeing her brings death. Take even greater care with the dog. If it sees you as it glances around, you yourself will be dead within a year.

Such is the legend. Many people will have heard of the notorious Lady Howard who murdered her four husbands. And as with many other tales, there isn't even a grain of truth buried deep within it. In the case of Lady Mary. it is more a whole intriguing story of love, treachery and revenge involving the richest families in Devon during the late sixteenth and seventeenth centuries. Lady Mary was a real, historical character, very wealthy, very well connected. But she has been called 'the Devil on Dartmoor' and 'the demon bride' now luring unsuspecting travellers to their deaths. She was neither. And all that remains of her mansion is the gatehouse which had led into a courtyard fronting the house with its fine porch and projecting wings. So what happened?

The story really begins with Lady Mary's father, John Fitz. Born in 1575, he was the only son of Sir John (1529-90) and Mary of Fitzford House. Like several of his forebears, Sir John had had a successful and lucrative career in the legal profession so not unnaturally had high expectations that his son would follow in his footsteps. It was not to be. Sir John died in January 1590 when young John was just 14. Five years later he married into nobility, to Bridget, sixth daughter of Sir William Courtenay of Powderham, 3rd Earl of Devon. Their daughter,

Mary, was born in August 1596. This was also the year John came of age, inheriting the extensive Fitz estates and becoming very wealthy – too much, too young, many were to say. By this time he seems to have been addicted to alcohol and was already an unpleasant and unpopular character, but now he began to develop symptoms of a psychotic paranoia, perhaps induced by alcohol abuse. He became increasingly unpredictable and confrontational, and in June 1599 when a trivial argument got out of hand he killed one of his few friends, Nicholas Slanning from Bickleigh – one tradition says he stabbed Slanning at the old gatehouse to Fitzford. John Fitz fled to France to escape arrest but returned some months later, following a royal pardon through the help of his wife's family connections. He was not in any way subdued. In a fit of pique he turned his wife and daughter out of the house, and they had to live with her parents at Powderham. Unrestrained, John and his associates wreaked havoc on Tavistock in alcohol-fuelled episodes of wanton destruction, fighting, breaking windows, quarrelling with anyone they met, and almost killing one of the town constables. Despite this, on the accession of James I in 1603 he was knighted, not for any service to his monarch but merely because of his social standing and wealth. However, in the summer of 1605 he was summoned to London to account for his behaviour to his family and to answer charges of unlawful murder. He expected a heavy fine but in his delusions believed his life was in danger, that the Slanning and Courtenay families were trying to kidnap and murder him. On the way, he became so deranged he killed a hotel keeper, before committing suicide by putting the hilt of his sword against a wall and impaling himself, twice. Some regarded it as just retribution. Mary Fitz, his daughter, was 9 years old.

The Earl of Northumberland, himself desperately short of money, was aware that John Fitz had left a huge estate and that his only daughter was still a child. He petitioned the king and for £465 bought the heiress's wardship, money he actually raised on her estate to be re-paid in instalments. As guardian he had complete control of the young Mary, received the rents from her estate, and could marry her off to whoever he wished. The Earl sent his younger brother Sir Alan Percy to cast his eye over her Fitzford, Walreddon and Okehampton properties, with instructions to make as much money as he could from selling the timber. At the age of 12, with no say in the matter, Mary was married to 31-year-old Sir Alan. Now the Percy family could get their hands on her fortune. As Mary was so young, the newly-weds didn't live together immediately – and they never did, for in November 1611 Mary's husband caught a severe chill while out hunting and died.

Now the Earl of Suffolk stepped in, with a scheme to get the wealthiest heiress in Devon for his third son, Sir Thomas Howard. But Mary put a stop to that. Though still a minor and a ward, she eloped with Thomas Darcy, Lord Darcy's son and her own age. But this, her one marriage for love, ended in tragedy when Darcy died just a few months later.

The last two of her marriages were again both about money, and both failed because she was no longer the innocent 9-year-old thrust into a venal world. Mary had learned how to assert herself, and refused to let her husbands milk her fortunes. The Earl of Suffolk hadn't given up, though. Mary was still not yet 16, and was married off to Sir Charles Howard, the Earl's fourth son. The couple actually went to live with the Earl and on September 21, 1613, her daughter, Elizabeth, was born. The child died soon afterwards, but a second daughter, Mary, quickly came along. Then on September 22. 1622, Sir Charles himself died, without a male heir.

Very wealthy and renowned for her wit as well as her beauty, Mary became an influential figure at the Court of Queen Henrietta Maria, wife of King Charles I. There she met the Duke of Buckingham – who had in mind a marriage of this rich widow to one of his own proteges, Richard Grenville, again with her fortunes uppermost in his mind. Mary agreed, and in 1628 Richard Grenville was made a baronet of Kilkhampton, his family seat in Cornwall. But Mary was fully aware what this meant as far as her fortune was concerned. Without a word to Grenville, advised by her land agent and steward, trusted friend and possibly lover, Puritan lawyer George Cutteford, she made what we would now call a 'pre-nuptial arrangement': she conveyed all her estates in trust, permitting her during her lifetime, whether married or not, to receive rents from her lands and dispose of them as she wished. With that safeguard, Mary brought her new husband to Fitzford. She quickly regretted it.

It was after their first child, Richard, was born in May, 1630, that Grenville discovered what his wife had done. To say he was annoyed is an understatement. His reaction was to resort to violence. He had no money or estate of his own. He couldn't accept he was dependent on her. Argument followed argument, living together became unbearable and household witnesses claimed he had smoked out her rooms, broken down doors, shredded her clothes and knocked her to the ground when she was pregnant, *"made her eyes blacke and blewe"*. Finally, in 1632 she escaped his brutal fists, rushing through the night to the custody of her former father-in-law, the Earl of Suffolk. But by doing so she initiated almost two decades of violent retribution. Mary was granted a divorce. She stayed on with the Suffolks, resuming the name of Howard. We know she gave birth to a son, George, but neither his date of birth nor his father are recorded. He may have been the Earl's but, as likely, George Cutteford may have been his father.

Ironically, Grenville was an outstanding soldier. During the Civil War, he was appointed King's General in the West. The King also granted him all Mary's estates. Two weeks later, he arrived in Tavistock. His opportunity had arrived, and he seized it: he had George Cutteford tortured to death in Lydford Gaol, took what he wanted from Fitzford house and demanded back rents from the tenants. Then he went to Plymouth and took command of the Royalist forces there. Nominally, he was in charge of Fitzford but neglectfully left only an inadequate garrison to defend it. The Parliamentarians attacked, Fitzford was surrendered and ransacked. Grenville stayed away. Despite this, in 1645 the King appointed him Sheriff of Devon. His sadistic vindictiveness increased, hanging soldiers and civilians arbitrarily at Lydford Gaol, insatiably extorting money, kidnapping for ransom, using war contributions for his own ends, profiteering, and even refusing to obey his own commanding officers. Consequently, in January 1646 he was arrested at Launceston and imprisoned in St Michael's Mount. Two months later, as Parliamentarians approached on March 3, 1646, he was allowed to escape. He never received the customary pardon from Parliament.

Lady Mary rushed to Fitzford. She found her mansion wrecked. With her beloved George, she set to repair the damage.

Grenville himself died in 1659, in Holland. His daughter Elizabeth looked after him at his end. Tradition says that Lady Mary detested Elizabeth but there is no documentation to support this. Mary did though make all her estates over to George, hoping he would live on at the ancestral home, but on September 17 1671, he too died. Mary was broken hearted. She died exactly one month later. In her will of October 14 1671 she left £500 to her daughter Mary, £1,000 to her daughter Elizabeth: they were in effect disinherited.

But the people of Tavistock were left with more than just an impression of Mary Howard's strong personality and imperious temper. She became legendary. The injustice is that she herself is the wronged party. The historical facts have skewed as stories which really revolved round other people, particularly her father, the last of her husbands and another lady with a similar name, were attributed to her. According to folklore, she murdered all four of her husbands. This is mistaken identity as the deeds of one Lady Howard, Frances, have landed on the shoulders of another, Mary. By coincidence, Frances was the daughter of the 1st Earl of Suffolk but also the central figure in a famous scandal during the reign of James I, when she was found guilty of poisoning her husband, 3rd Earl of Essex. However, it is our Lady Howard who now rides a coach made from her husbands' bones on a futile nightly journey to expiate her crimes, never to rest from the adversity that was her life. According to the legend, if you see the coach, there is death. Perhaps there is some truth in that. Lady Mary knew all about death. She did outlive her four husbands, though she never murdered any of them. Most of her own children died young, which was not uncommon at the time. But if you do see her, you can take consolation that her only 'crime' was to cut off her daughters' inheritance.

Oxenham Manor, South Zeal

- EX20 2RQ

A booklet was published In 1641 with the title *A True Relation Of An Apparition*. It described one of the strangest family traditions in Devon. The scene was a remote farm, Oxenham Manor, at the foot of Cosdon, the huge hill that dominates the north-east corner of Dartmoor.

This was the home of the Oxenhams from the 13th century until 1814. Stone pillars leaning in front of the house are inscribed with the date 1714, the year in which they renovated and enlarged it. And during this time they became famous for a sequence of apparitions, always involving a white-breasted bird: if one of them saw it, their fate was sealed. Admittedly, some of those Oxenhams were already on their deathbeds when the white bird fluttered by but there have been sightings by healthy members who met untimely deaths.

The first record of these events came from a branch of the family who lived in the Manor in Zeal Monachorum, headed by James Oxenham. James had a large family until in 1635 his eldest son, 22-years-old John, from all accounts a strong, healthy, tall ("being in height of body sixe fotte and an halfe") young man unexpectedly fell ill and died soon afterwards. Only two days before, he had seen a white bird hovering above him. Other people had seen it and told both the vicar and the bishop about the 'fetch', a personification. Now, on his deathbed the bird mysteriously came into the room and fluttered over John again. Within two days, Thomazine, his sister-in-law, wife of his brother James, also fell ill and died: again the white bird flew into her room just before her death. Two days later still, John's eight-year-old sister, Rebeccah, also saw this white bird, and she too died. Whatever the sickness was, possibly some sort of contagious plague, it took two more infants, including Thomazine's baby, and each time the white bird had been there. In the case of four others who caught the illness but recovered, the bird had not been involved. Only then did the family remember that a white bird had been seen when John's grandmother, Grace, had been on her deathbed in 1618.

There is only oral evidence to support the bird's most dramatic appearance, but the story continues with Margaret, heiress to the property who was pledged to marry a neighbouring landowner, Bertram. However, as a consequence of an accident, he became mentally deranged. For some time, Margaret was upset by this, until she was courted by Sir John of Roxamcave. It was Christmas Eve. James Oxenham was giving a banquet for every-one in the area in honour of his daughter, Margaret, who was to marry on Boxing Day. James rose to his feet. He spoke of his daughter, of how he would miss her, but was delighted with her choice of husband. The diners listened attentively. James faltered in his speech. He sank back in his chair, knocking a glass of wine which spread on the cloth – like blood. Was the emotion of the occasion too much for him? It wasn't that. He had seen the white-breasted bird fly high above the table and twice round Margaret. He feared what it foretold. But he decided to say nothing about it. Perhaps if he had Margaret might have been warned to be careful. On her wedding morning on Boxing Day, arrangements went ahead. The church at South Tawton was filled to the doors. Margaret walked up the aisle to meet her groom at the altar. The vicar began the service – and from behind a pillar the rejected Bertram rushed and stabbed a knife into her breast. Before anyone could move, he withdrew the dagger and plunged it into his own heart. Scarlet blood spurted onto Margaret's dress. Both Margaret and Bertram died instantly.

Fairly continuously down the years there have been reports of the white bird's activities. In 1743, William Oxenham, aged sixty-four, was feeling slightly unwell when he saw the white bird fluttering outside his bedroom window. Defiantly, he shouted that *"he would cheat the bird"*: he might be feeling sick, but not that sick – yet within three days he was dead just the same. Then sometime between 1810 and 1821, at Sidmouth, another member of the family died in a house which is now Sidlands. People present knew nothing of the legend but they did see a white bird fly across the room. Later, in 1873, a Mr N G Oxenham died in Kensington. His nephew, Revd Henry Oxenham, testified that a week before his uncle's death he had seen a white bird fluttering outside the window. His daughter and her friend, again knowing nothing of the tradition, opened the window and both saw a white bird, larger than a pigeon, perched on a tree outside, which some workmen were trying to frighten off. Later, in 1892, the bird was seen by another of the Oxenhams and soon afterwards his father died.

Although by the mid-twentieth century, family members were becoming more sceptical, the bird continued its sombre activity. There are several recently recorded occasions when the white bird was seen around the deathbeds of an Oxenham. So just what is the creature? Is it a long-repressed family totem? Or a mental projection from one of the original family influencing each generation? A collective memory passed from generation to generation but shared only within the one family? A banshee? Or a truly ghostly bird?

Highwayman Inn, Sourton

- EX20 4HN

Whichever way you look at it, the Highwayman Inn at Sourton is unique. Drinkers come to sample its fine ales, others because it is Britain's most haunted inn. You have to see it to believe it: part pirate ship, part church, part museum, part junk yard, with the old Launceston to Tavistock coach as the entrance porch and Old Mother Hubbard's shoe in the car park, it was created over a period of 40 years by John 'Buster' and Rita Jones and is now run by their daughter, Sally, and son-in-law. The site itself is auspicious. Dating back to 1282, it is close to a ley line, has changed names many times from the Golden Fleece to New Inn, but became the Highwayman when John and Rita took over in 1959 after they heard stories of how three highwaymen, named Fowley, Huggins and Creber, had been active in the area at one time, offering romantic notions of them emerging from the mists of mysterious Dartmoor.

Today, the building is alive with ghostly activity, ranging from spectral footfalls to full apparitions. The one most frequently seen is that of Samuel the Cavalier. He dresses in green with a large feather in his hat, is always friendly and usually appears around 10am in the Galleon Room, from where he walks through a wall where a door used to lead to the old stable block. Why here? He has been associated with the Battle of Sourton Cross, which took place a mile away during the Civil Wars. There are other ghosts, too: a licentious woman in a mop cap, a man identified by a medium as 'Joseph' who sits at the bar, and a sea captain named Grenville. There is also a figure in a dark coat who came into the pub one day in 2002, the doorbell rang, but then he walked into one of the bars and disappeared. Visitors taking photographs in the Galleon Room have captured orbs coming out of the door, which belonged to the *Diana* before she sank in 1817 taking 16 souls with her. There is a story of buried treasure on the premises, but no one has identified the exact spot yet! Not all the ghosts can be seen by humans. The Ghost Research Foundation carried out its first official investigation here in October 2001 and identified a variety of colourful spectres that flit unseen among the living guests. A later visitor filmed the Victorian Room and was staggered when he got home to see he had caught a foggy moving image on his video.

Strange things have also been seen and felt at Cobweb Hall across the road, which was originally the village's Victorian church hall but is now part of the inn and let out as a holiday home.

Widecombe-in-the-Moor
Old Inn - EX20 4HN   Jay's Grave - map ref 731799

Everyone knows Widecombe-in-the-Moor. Almost at the centre of Dartmoor, made famous by the folk song about its Fair, the village is an essential stop for tourists who come to see what all the fuss was about.

But it also has ghosts. The poor horse in the song has good reason to re-appear as one, galloping over the hills near the village. Just imagine the scene. Seven hulking country boys living almost twenty miles away decide to visit Widecome Fair. But this was long before cars or public transport so they borrow Tom Pearce's old grey mare, scramble onto her back and expect her to carry them all the way. Why? Just so they might drink themselves into a stupor? Such a demand on a poor horse just wasn't reasonable. She collapsed and died. But what really may have happened. For a start, surely they didn't think they could all ride on a single horse? Or did they borrow her to pull them in a cart or gig? Having had a busy time at the Fair, now 'owdered up', did their carriage overturn on the return journey, killing the poor mare? The characters who caused her premature death with their drunken capers are all named in the song, but the old grey mare remains anonymous. In revenge her bones can be heard rattling nearby. This must be true as Uncle Tom Cobley signed the 1963 first day cover of the British Fairs issue of stamps – and stole Tavistock's thunder on the stamp depicting their Goosey Fair!

The picturesque pub at the centre of Widecombe is the Old Inn. Dating from the 14th century, it looks every bit as ancient as its name suggests though it has been expanded over the years to accommodate the constant invasion of tourists. Despite a major fire in 1977, it has two ghosts, though we haven't come across any explanation for them. The first is 'Old Harry'. Some say he was murdered here. His favourite haunt is the new dining-room (once the scullery) between the bar and the kitchen. Mid-afternoon is his preferred time, when he walks into a room with just one door and whose walls are solid granite – which he walks through. Because he is so lifelike he doesn't scare anyone. Unlike the standard, see-through apparition, he seems very solid, three-dimensional and real. Indeed, until he walks through the wall and disappears, people don't even realise he is a ghost.

There is also a child who cries endlessly for hours in an empty upstairs bedroom. Her heart-rending sobs have affected many visitors, but as soon as the door is opened the pitiful weeping stops: no-one is there. In 1993, a TV crew brought a medium who, without any prior knowledge, located the right part of the building and informed them that the poor, sobbing child was 'Kathy'. Before then and since, many guests have sensed a distinct and definite 'presence'. These cries might however be the supernatural echoes of Mary 'Kitty' Jay and her child.

Mary Jay was born in 1790. Immediately afterwards she was taken to Wolborough Work House in Newton Abbot, where records show her as an orphaned 'female child', no name, no date of birth. In such cases, surnames were allocated by the staff in alphabetical order. Next in line was 'J', so the baby was registered as 'Jay' with the Christian name 'Mary'. Mary Jay stayed at the Work House for several years and when she was old enough was given the job of supervising younger children. According to the *Apprentices' Register*, when she reached her teens she was sent to work for a farmer at Canna Ford Farm, Manaton, as an 'apprentice' – a euphemism for general drudging inside the house and labouring in the fields. The work was back-breaking, days were long, and the most she could expect was the rare luxury of a reasonable meal and warm clothing. Then for some unknown reason in late September 1806 she hanged herself in one of the outbuildings.

Folklore steps in here to tell us why: she was pregnant by the farmer's son who gave her the nickname 'Kitty' but who reneged on his promise to marry her. To Kitty, any attention had been better than none, any security to be snatched. But those were hard times. She quickly learned her value to the farmer. She was thrown out. Branded as a slut, she had nowhere to go, no family to turn to, no one to help her and her unborn child conceived out of wedlock, no means of support and no chance of finding any form of employment. She didn't want to return to the Work House in disgrace. So in desperation she took her own life. Vicars at Widecombe, North Bovey and Manaton refused to bury her in their churchyards. Worse for Kitty, these were less enlightened times than now. Until 1823, the law denied suicides burial in consecrated ground. They had to be buried at the nearest crossroads – with a stake through their bodies so their troubled spirit could not find its way back to their village. So not for Kitty to lie amongst a weathered assembly of mossy tombstones. The poor soul was buried by the wayside, late at night on a lonely, windswept part of Dartmoor overlooked by Hound Tor, at an intersection of a road and a moorland miners' track where the three parishes meet – to ensure none of them acquired any responsibility. She was attended only by three men paid by the Parish to dig the grave and cover her body, mourned by none and often engulfed in cold, damp, swirling mist. Such was the fate of Kitty Jay.

In 1860, some of the employees of James Bryant of Prospect, Hedge Barton, near Hound Tor, were mending a stretch of road. As one of them was cleaning out the ditches, his spade hit something hard in a rough mound. When he separated this from the roots and stones, he noticed it was a piece of bone. He was about to throw it to one side as just another bit of some moorland animal when his companions dug further – and discovered more bones in what was a rough grave. This they reported to Mr Bryant, who had the bones examined: they were identified as human, and moreover from a young woman. Locals remembered how an orphan girl had hanged herself and been buried here. James Bryant ordered the bones to be put in a box and re-buried at the spot, raising the mound as it is today. Then in the 1970s the Dartmoor National Park Authority had kerb stones put around the grave to protect it from damage by cattle and sheep.

It wasn't long before strange events began to occur at 'Jay's Grave'. On moonlit nights a dark figure could be seen kneeling beside the sad little mound of earth, head bowed and face buried in its hands – and it still is. The figure is enveloped in a long, heavy black cloak and hood, its outlines are ill-defined so no-one can tell if it is male or female, or even if it is the ghost of Kitty herself. Is it the spirit of one of those who hounded her to her death? Is it the duplicitous farmer's son, doomed for his mendacity to keep eternal vigil over the spot where his victim and her unborn child lie buried? People passing by have seen 'something', the troubled spirit Kitty Jay perhaps, hovering over the grave. It has even been caught in car headlights.

Then something else started to happen. Every day, fresh flowers appeared on the little grave. No matter what time of year, no matter how bad the weather, primroses, daffodils, tulips, bluebells, wild marguerites, heather or rhododendron flowers from the wall of Hedge Barton, were left in a jar carefully located at the head of the grave. At

Christmas there was holly and evergreens. Such a caring act created its own mystery. No-one knew who did it. No-one was seen leaving the flowers. Were they really placed there by hands unknown? Again, folklore stepped in. Some people said it was the work of piskies, tending the grave forever out of sympathy. Or in modern times had the grave become a place of pilgrimage? Many people think it was Beatrice Chase, a prolific Dartmoor writer who lived nearby, but she died in 1955 – so who continued after her? The flowers even appeared during the 2001 Foot and Mouth epidemic when the Moor was almost completely closed to visitors: so it looks likely it was either piskies or some kindly neighbour who took over the job. Now a plethora of items have been placed on the grave by visitors – surely piskies don't use silk or plastic flowers, do they?

Kitty Jay's tragedy touched many hearts. The story inspired John Galsworthy's 1916 'The Apple Tree' and Lois Deacon's 1973 novel *Angel From Your Door*. An album of folk songs by composer Seth Lakeman has the ballad of Kitty Jay as its title. So the fascination remains. And the hauntings continue.

Kitty Jay is not the only person to have been buried on Dartmoor, but none have attracted the same attention. George Stephens' grave is on the high, open moor at Sidford, a few miles from Peter Tavy – but there is no mystery over his grave, his death or fresh flowers appearing every day. He was a sheep stealer, the last to be hanged in Salcombe Regis parish, where the 'Elephant Tree' marks the site of the old gallows. But woven round this is the lore that George met and fell in love with a local girl but was rejected by her parents as unworthy of their daughter. Inconsolable, he took his own life by eating deadly nightshade – though one version of the story says he poisoned the girl first so their souls could be together forever. As a suicide, he was buried at this bleak, windswept crossroads on the edge of the moors. At the very moment he was lowered into this peaty grave a white sheet hanging on a washing line nearby was blown into the sky and was never seen again. His ghost can, though, on dark nights.

Hayne Manor, Stowford
- EX20 4DB

In the heart of glorious countryside on the edge of the Dartmoor National Park, not far from the River Tamar, Hayne Manor is a beautiful place – and is home to several ghosts. One involves a murder mystery solved by a farmer's vivid dreams, another relates to a cursed field.

The Hayne estate was acquired by the Harris family in the early 16th century. For the next 300 years they lived here and were responsible for the house being redesigned and rebuilt in Gothic Revival style by the architect Sir Jeffry Wyatville in 1810, and extended further in 1865. Over the next century it went through a phase of less careful owners, so by the 1980s sadly had become derelict and the estate divided. Fortunately for us – and the ghost – it was bought and thoroughly restored by Lord Stockton, chairman of Macmillan Publishers, politician and grandson of former Prime Minister Harold Macmillan. It has since been sold again and remains a private mansion and estate.

Our story begins in 1891. This was the year of the 'Great Blizzard'. Snow began to fall on March 9 and for six weeks the whole country was paralysed by huge drifts driven by gale-force winds. Like everywhere else, Hayne was blanketed, owners and staff unable to get in or out. At that time, Hayne Manor was owned by Lord Conway, but it was his daughter and son-in-law, Sir George and Lady Harris, who lived here. Lady Harris herself haunts one of the bedrooms. Amongst her many staff, she employed a page, always dressed immaculately in smart livery, silver buttons on his jacket, his lady's insignia on his collar and sleeves, whose job was to sit in a corridor near her private apartments ever ready to respond to her imperious commands. Only when Lady Harris had gone to sleep was he allowed to climb into his own bed in a small room adjoining the housekeeper's room. Close by, the butler slept in the pantry, where the Manor's silver and plate was kept. He had served the family for many years, had an irreproachable character and was a favourite of Lord Conway, so well-placed to look after the family's valuables.

One morning later in that year, Mrs Harris called for her page. Fourteen-years-old Richard Tarwell, didn't respond. The staff looked for him – but he was missing. And so was a considerable quantity of the family's silver. Hayne Manor had been burgled. There was no obvious clue about any robbery, how anyone had got into the house, but someone must have. First, the butler, Richard Morris, was questioned by the police. He was able to help immediately with a vivid description of how had been roused by a noise, had gone to the plate-room where he was seized from behind, tied, gagged and threatened he would be killed if he made any sound or attempted to move. But among those attacking him, he did recognise the page. The housekeeper confirmed much of what the butler had said. She had been wakened too, but was too frightened to move until all went quiet – when she found Mr Morris tied and gagged in the plate-room, and managed to release him. Not surprisingly, everyone thought the page had taken a major part in the robbery and had run away, or at the most generous interpretation had been forcibly taken by the thieves.

Mrs Harris was distraught at the loss of her 'best' page though everyone else was more concerned about the theft of the goods. Nonetheless, she initiated a search: pawnbrokers and premises of known receivers of stolen goods in Exeter and Plymouth were searched but none of the articles turned up. Nor did any information about the page. The police,too, drew a blank.

Years passed, by degrees the circumstances of the theft became a mystery, the incident became part of the family's folklore, but no-one could solve it and no clues came to light. Until that is, at one of the annual Court Leet or rent days, held each October on the Hayne estate. Over the years, certain traditions had grown up around the event. Tenants living some distance away in Devon and Cornwall would stay overnight at Hayne on the eve of the Leet, pay their rent next day and attend a dinner given by their landlord, Lord Conway, and on the third day return home. On this particular occasion, two of the tenants, Mr Weare of Tiverton and Mr Bonifant of Torrington, occupied the same room. In the middle of the night, Mr Bonifant awoke suddenly, trembling. He had had a most vivid dream in which a ghostly page boy had appeared. The apparition told him that in the night he had been woken by a noise and had seen the butler and housekeeper packing the plate into a hamper, that they realised he was watching and had promptly murdered him, then forced his body through the iron bars of the window of the housekeeper's room, carried it to the terrace, on to the Chinese summer house, and buried it behind a wall at the foot of a huge yew tree.

Mr Bonifant woke his companion to tell him what had happened. The other farmer laughed at the story. Obviously, too much of the free ale had been drunk. He should just go back to sleep. But as Mr Bonifant dropped off, the same dream re-occurred. Clearly frightened, he got up and for the remainder of the night stayed awake in an armchair. Later that day, the two tenant farmers paid their rent, and strolled into the park surrounding the house. They walked where they had never been before and as they approached the terrace Mr Bonifant recognised various spots from his dream – a fact which only increased his fear.

That night, Bonifant had the same dream, repeating details of the robbery and the murder, only this time the page's apparition beckoned him onto the terrace, to the Chinese summer house and the large yew tree. He was clearly terrified when he woke his colleague. At this point, Mr Weare too became uncomfortable and suggested that before they left they should mention it to Mrs Harris's husband. Mr Harris's immediate response was that they were being ridiculous, but as they were both so clearly distressed he promised to do something about it before they left to go home. He then wrote a note to his solicitor in Launceston, asking him to delay the messenger (who Mr Harris ensured was Morris, the butler) by saying that he required a reply the same day. After the butler had set off for Launceston, Mr Harris, a gardener and two labourers with spades and picks, along with Mr Bonifant, went to find where the body, allegedly, had been buried. Mr Bonifant pointed out the exact spot where they should dig. There the men found human remains – later identified as those of the page.

What are we to make of this? That a man should dream the same thing three times must be unusual. Even if one accepts that the second two dreams had already been imprinted in his mind, what caused the first? The farmer had been coming to Hayne for years and had talked over the murder every time. It was a continual topic of conversation – it was part of the lore of the place – but nothing had occurred to clear it up. Even when the incident was fresh, and talk about it was excitedly, wildly speculative, no vision had occurred to him, no dream. But when the circumstances were fading from people's memories, he had experienced one, clear and detailed – not once, but three times! What are the probabilities of a single mind weaving together a long and precise succession of facts that actually took place? Surely, this was not a recurring dream. It was more than that.

Richard Morris was arrested and committed to Launceston Gaol, was tried in Exeter for the crime and hanged. The housekeeper had left the family some years earlier and moved to Exeter, where she had died – with her secret. But the page's ghost has haunted the spot every since.

The phenomenon of the accursed field is in the estate itself. Where there is now just the remains of an oak plantation, there used to be a productive field under annual cultivation. At some time around 1800, long before the introduction of heavy machinery, harvests here were reaped by men using scythes and reaping hooks which they kept particularly sharp. It was hard, hot, dusty labour but for some reason we don't know, two of these men fell out. They quarrelled noisily. Their colleagues couldn't pacify them or get them to concentrate on their work. One really lost his temper and threw his hook at the other, catching him in his neck and killing him. Move on to the next year, and an almost identical incident occurred. The estate employees and temporary labourers from the village were so shocked at this double tragedy that they refused to carry on with their work: no matter how he tried, the owner couldn't persuade the men to cultivate the field as normally. It became neglected. Oak trees were planted instead and left to grow.

In 1963, however, the owner decided to return the field into cultivation. The oaks were cleared and sawn for logs and firewood. But as this was going on the blade of the circular saw disintegrated and a splinter hit a young worker standing alongside the machine, and killed him. Surely this was more than coincidence: the young man was a direct descendant the the first man who was killed.

Postbridge – PL20 6TH

On June 19, 1921, the *Western Daily News* reported the inquest into the death of Dr Ernest H Helby, the Medical Officer at Dartmoor Prison. In March, Dr Helby had been killed in a motor-cycle accident near Postbridge. No other vehicles were involved, but his two passengers, his own daughter and her friend who was daughter of a Governor at the prison, were unhurt. They gave evidence to the Coroner that just outside Postbridge the doctor suddenly seemed to be having difficulty controlling the bike, had shouted to them to jump clear and seconds later had crashed into a ditch, with the engine literally detaching itself from the bike's frame. The Coroner heard how the bike had been in good order, was serviced recently, that Dr Helby was an experienced, careful motor-cyclist, knew the road well, the weather conditions were good and no-one was in a hurry. A verdict of 'Accidental Death' was recorded. The facts are stark. There was no rational explanation for this fatality. So what had happened? What had caused such an unusual accident?

Actually, this was not the first – nor the last – time something strange had happened here. Since 1910, drivers and cyclists had been reporting unusual accidents on the B3212 between Postbridge and Two Bridges in the Archerton region of Dartmoor. Mostly, these involved their vehicle having jolted unexpectedly or swerved violently off the road onto the verges, and always as if an unseen pair of hands had wrenched the steering wheel – or even the wheels of the car – out of their control. Cyclists had had their handlebars wrenched out of their hands forcing them into the ditch. Even ponies and traps had been forced off the road onto the verges. Indeed, only a few weeks after Dr Helby's death, at exactly the same spot a coach driver lost control and several passengers were injured when they were thrown out of their seats – and the driver stated that he had felt as if invisible hands had wrenched the steering wheel from his control. A few weeks later still, on the dull, foggy Friday of August 26, 1921, a young army Captain reported how an invisible 'pair of large, muscular, hairy hands' had clamped over his and forced his motorcycle off the road onto the verge at the same place. He escaped with shock and scratches. But he too was a very experienced rider.

Now the national newspapers took interest. The *Daily Mail* of October 14 and 15, 1921, reported all three motoring accidents near the gate of Archerton Drive on Nine Mile Hill. And speculation began. Were the incidents connected to the ghosts of highwaymen who had roamed Dartmoor, or to ghostly processions of people who had made their way regularly across the bleak Lych Way's 13th-century clapper bridge crossing the East Dart River, carrying the coffin with them for burials in Lydford?

Local authors got involved, too. One described how while driving near Postbridge a pair of hands had gripped the steering wheel of his car so he had to fight for control and narrowly avoided a crash – when the 'hands' disappeared as inexplicably as they had appeared. Many locals were sceptical. They put the accidents down to visitors being unfamiliar with the area, or driving too fast down narrow roads. The pervading atmosphere was generally eerie, which has an affect on visitors, and it is easy to become disoriented in the low mists which often occur. Then in 1924, a lady caravanning with her husband in the ruins of Powder Mills, half a mile north of the B3212, saw a pair of 'hairy hands' creeping across the grass towards them and up the window, trying to get in, but retreated when she made the sign of the cross – though she did feel that these disembodied hands were 'evil' and intent on doing her harm. Soon afterwards, a car was found upturned in the ditch, the driver dead at the wheel. Then on September 12, 1926, another national newspaper reported a further accident, again involving a motorcyclist caused by an 'Evil Ghost of a Moor Land Road'. Passers-by carried the young driver to a nearby cottage where when he regained consciousness he reported having been seized and thrown violently from his bike.

It was now time for officialdom to take notice. Several investigations were held. Civil engineers concluded that the accidents were most likely caused by the camber of the road's surface, which reached dangerous levels in places. The road was repaired and altered – but the accidents and even fatalities continued. In 1961, a young man was found dead underneath his car at this spot, and though forensic experts carried out a thorough examination of both the body and the car, nothing could explain the accident. In 1991, a doctor from Somerset turned his car over at the spot. Like others, he said it was as if some 'force' had sent it out of control, and that the atmosphere within the car suddenly became deathly cold, literally paralysing him. To this present day, people tell of spectral hands grabbing steering wheels or an evil presence inside the car which makes driving erratic. The latest report seems to be on June 6, 2006, when a visitor saw the 'hairy hands' at Higher Cherrybrook Bridge, stopped and took a photograph of them swinging on the barbed wire fence! But someone else stole them!

So what are we left with? 'Rational' explanations have varied from drivers having drunk a little more than was good for them at local pubs to the adverse camber still causing the problems to the road being subject to patches of black ice (though most of the accidents occur in summer) to visitors driving too fast on roads they do not know to wandering ponies, cattle and sheep forcing drivers to take emergency avoiding action. Actually, none of these explain the phenomena. These have been reported time and again as a pair of hairy hands trying to take control of vehicles – cars, coaches, bicycles, motor-cycles. So what and where are they? Or is there another explanation?

In the early hours of the misty morning of April 14, 1969, a family were driving from Postbridge towards Moretonhampstead when they came to a sharp corner. Suddenly, another car shot round the bend on the wrong side of the road. The driver swerved frantically to avoid it and ended up in the ditch – but the car never passed. Trying to restart, they found the battery was flat – but they had just driven for several miles and it should have been fully charged. They arranged through the AA for the car to be towed to the garage, where mechanics found the motor to be completely drained of power – and the garage owner confirmed that no other car had passed that way for several hours. Moreover, the AA man told how there had been a fatal accident at that very spot where the phantom car appeared, and that ever since similar apparitions had been seen by drivers.

Is there a connection? Has some kind of malignant influence been created in the area, which is still with us?